ISBN 978-1-334-62941-9
PIBN 10767692

English
Français
Deutsche
Italiano
Español
Português

www.forgottenbooks.com

Mythology Photography **Fiction**
Fishing Christianity **Art** Cooking
Essays Buddhism Freemasonry
Medicine **Biology** Music **Ancient
Egypt** Evolution Carpentry Physics
Dance Geology **Mathematics** Fitness
Shakespeare **Folklore** Yoga Marketing
Confidence Immortality Biographies
Poetry **Psychology** Witchcraft
Electronics Chemistry History **Law**
Accounting **Philosophy** Anthropology
Alchemy Drama Quantum Mechanics
Atheism Sexual Health **Ancient History**
Entrepreneurship Languages Sport
Paleontology Needlework Islam
Metaphysics Investment Archaeology
Parenting Statistics Criminology
Motivational

CONTENTS.

TABLE I —

(Compiled from the monthly Meteoro

Serial No.	MONTH.	NORMAL MEAN.	1892-93.	1893-94.	1894-95.	1895-96.
		Inches.	Inches.	Inches.	Inches.	Inches.
	TOTAL ...	63·50	85·43	69·17	71·52	56·31
1	April ...	0·62	Nil	0·30	0·10	1·42
2	May ...	1·19	0·08	2·90	0·11	0·63
3	June ...	10·44	10·57	14·20	12·16	17·72
4	July ...	17·35	32·58	16·41	19·12	14·79
5	August ...	18·26	19·00	9·63	24·29	15·01
6	September	8·82	9 58	20·63	5·27	4·10
7	October ...	3·04	2·78	4·15	6·61	2·52
8	November	0·55	0·05	0·52	0·96	Nil
9	December	0·39	Nil	Nil	Nil	Nil
10	January	0·73	1·58	0·01	0·17	Nil
11	February	1·12	6·98	0·40	1·38	Nil
12	March ...	0·99	2·23	0·02	1·35	0·12

TABLE II.—ARE

(Compiled from the following Census Tables :—Imperial Table and Table of Statistics prep

Serial No.	STATE.	Area in square miles.	Number of		POPULATION IN 1901.		
			Towns.	Villages.	Total.	Male.	Female.
	1	2	3	4	5	6	
	TOTAL	16,014	...	4,603	1,001,429	506,759	494,670
1	Chāng Bhakār	904	...	117	19,548	10,003	9,545
2	Koreā	1,631	...	250	35,113	17,946	17,16
3	Surgujā	6,089	...	1,372	351,011	177,961	173,05
4	Udaipur	1,052	...	196	45,391	23,107	22,28
5	Jashpur	1,948	...	566	132,114	66,647	65,46
6	Gāngpur	2,492	...	806	238,896	121,492	117,40
7	Bonai	1,296	...	217	38,277	20,001	18,27
8	Kharsāwān	153	...	263	36,540	17,768	18,77
9	Saraikelā	440	...	816	104,539	51,832	52,70

NOTE.—The figures for area which differ slightly from those adopted in the Census Re
on the basis of t

TABLE III.

CHOTA NAGPUR TRIBUTARY

(STATES GAZETTEER.)

STATISTICS, 1901-02.

Bengal.
= Bengal district gazetteer

TABLE IV.—RELIGION AND

(Compiled from the Census Provincial Table II of 190

Serial No.	STATE.		Hindu.	Animist.	Musalmān.
	1		2	3	4
	TOTAL ...		*615,454*	*375,478*	*8,614*
1	Chāng Bhakār	... ...	19,516	1	31
2	Koreā	... ...	24,430	10,395	288
3	Surgujā	... ...	204,228	142,783	3,999
4	Udaipur	... ...	41,373	3,897	121
5	Jashpur	... ...	69,473	61,475	1,154
6	Gāngpur	... ...	146,549	88,949	1,640
7	Bonai	... ...	26,371	11,745	69
8	Kharsāwān	... ...	19,864	16,277	399
9	Saraikelā	... ...	63,650	39,956	913

TABLE V.—CASTE

(Compiled from the Cen

Serial No.	CASTE, TRIBE OR RACE NUMBERING MORE THAN 25,000.		Chāng Bhakār.	Koreā.	Surgujā.	Udaipur.
	1		2	3	4	5
	HINDU.					
1	Ahīr and Goālā	... ...	1,882	3,397	29,681	2,485
2	Bhuiyā	... ...	340	1,974	6,855	2,132
3	Gond	... ...	5,252	9,682	83,134	4,135
4	Ho	... ...	4,704	542	68	—
5	Kaur	... ...	1,383	3,456	28,799	15,895
6	Kharia	... ...	—	—	122	—
7	Korwā	... ...	143	...	15,756	—
8	Mundā	... ...	290	113	6,506	1,945
9	Orāon	... ...	1	465	29,276	3,325
10	Pān (Pānika)	... ...	1,444	2,134	38,482	2,323
11	Sonthal	... ...	272	127	5,361	1,729

TABLE V

EDUCATION IN 1901.

nd from the Census Tabulation Register of Table VIII.)

I O N .			EDUCATION.		
Christian.	Others.		Number of persons able to read and write.	Number of persons able to read and write English.	Serial No.
5	6		7	8	
1,876			8,340	173	
	...		47	1	1
	...		84	3	2
...	...		914	37	3
	...		239	2	4
12	...		862	9	5
1,758	...		3,158	30	6
92			373	7	7
			1,057	35	8
13	7		1,616	49	9

TRIBE OR RACE.

Provincial Table III of 1901.)

S T A T E .						
Jashpur.	Gāngpur.	Bonai.	Kharsāwān.	Saraikela.	Total.	Serial No.
6	7	8	9	10	11	
8,576	4,587	407	2,507	5,283	58,178	1
4,333	23,595	6,428	1,966	6,499	53,817	2
3,113	37,242	5,707	895	3,160	153,209	3
135	5,551	4,500	15,609	20,683	51,806	4
6,563	1,833	...	...	...	60,369	5
3,222	25,838	2,721	...	...	31,903	6
9,727	450	265	...	229	26,570	7
4,166	18,569	3,671	42	105	35,397	8
47,345	47,457	1,526	366	132	729,993	9
493	2,550	3,358	26	214	43,584	10
9	982	29	889	19,933	29,346	11

(Blank.)

TABLE VII.—Blank.

TABLE VIII.—Blank.

TABLE IX.—PRICES IN SEERS PER RUPEE.

(Compiled from figures supplied by the Commissioner, Chota Nāgpur Division).

PARTICULARS.		DURING THE LAST FORTNIGHT OF MARCH									
		1893.	1894.	1895.	1896.	1897.	1898.	1899.	1900.	1901.	19..
		s. c.	s. c.	s. c.	s. c.	s. c.	s. c.	s. c.	s. c.	s. c.	s. c.
CHANG BHAKAR.	Wheat	16 0	12 0	20 0	...	7 0	14 0	16 0	Not available.	.	16
	Rice...	22 0	20 0	20 0	15 0	7 0	30 0	40 0			25
	Gram	30 0	30 0	30 0	...	7 0	15 0	20 0			15
	Salt ...	Not available.									
KOREA	Wheat	35 0	37 0	27 8	15 0	9 0	12 0	20 0	10 0	26 0	13
	Rice...	35 0	37 0	25 0	16 0	8 0	10 0	20 0	10 0	30 0	14
	Gram	40 0	40 0	30 0	15 0	10 0	12 0	16 0	10 0	26 0	22
	Salt ...	Not available.									
SURGUJA...	Wheat	16 0	16 0	14 0	14 0	10 0	14 0	14 0	11 0	13 0	16
	Rice...	18 0	18 0	18 0	15 0	14 0	21 0	37 0	15 0	30 0	30
	Gram	22 0	22 0	18 0	15 0	13 0	18 0	30 0	20 0	29 0	23
	Salt ...	Not available.									
UDAIPUR...	Wheat	26 0	25 0	25 0	16 0	10 0	12 0	20 0			
	Rice...	33 0	32 0	32 0	16 0	15 0	22 0	60 0	40 0	40 0	40
	Gram	32 0	32 0	32 0	12 0	12 0	19 0	40 0			
	Salt ...	Not available.									
JASHPUR...	Wheat	13 0	14 0	14 0	10 0	10 0	12 0	13 0	10 0	11 0	
	Rice...	24 0	24 0	24 0	16 0	16 0	24 0	40 0	16 0	28 0	
	Gram	13 0	14 0	14 0	12 0	13 0	13 0	16 0	12 0	14 0	
	Salt ...	Not available.									
GANGPUR	Wheat	10 0	19 0	...	...	7 0	10 0	13 0	12 0	12 0	...
	Rice...	16 0	24 0	24 0	16 0	12 0	16 0	16 0	10 0	16 0	16
	Gram	12 0	18 0	18 0	14 0	6 0	10 0	16 0	8 0	10 0	
	Salt ...	Not available.									
BONAI	Wheat	Not available.	16 0	...	...	...	...	...			10
	Rice...		16 0	24 0	24 0	16 0	24 0	24 0	12 0	11 0	16
	Gram		16 0	16 0	16 0	...	16 0	16 0	10 0	10 0	10
	Salt ...	Not available.									
KHARSAWAN	Wheat	12 0	12 0	12 0	12 0	10 0	10 0	16 0	16 0	12 0	10
	Rice...	14 0	14 0	16 0	14 0	10 0	16 0	24 0	16 0	20 0	16
	Gram	12 0	12 0	8 0	12 0	10 0	10 0	16 0	16 0	12 0	12
	Salt ...	Not available.									
SARAIKELA	Wheat	12 0	16 0	15 0	14 0	9 0	11 0	16 0	12 0	12 0	10
	Rice...	16 0	17 0	23 0	25 0	10 0	16 0	24 0	14 0	16 0	15
	Gram	12 0	12 0	14 0	24 0	10 0	11 0	16 0	12 0	10 0	12
	Salt ...	Not available.									

TABLE X.—DAILY WAGES.

FOR	DURING THE LAST FORTNIGHT OF MARCH									
	1893.	1894.	1895.	1896.	1897.	1898.	1899.	1900.	1901.	1902.
	A. P.	A. P.	A. P.	A. P.	A. P.	Rs. A. P.	Rs. A. P.	A. P.	A. P.	A. P.
CHANG BHAKAR STATE.										
Superior mason	...	...	...	...	...	...	...	...	...	...
Common ,,	...	...	...	...	...	...	...	...	...	...
Superior carpenter	...	...	...	...	...	...	...	...	...	...
Common ,,	...	...	...	...	...	...	...	...	...	...
Cooly	1 0	1 0	1 0	1 0	1 0	0 1 0	0 1 0	1 0	1 0	1 0
Woman	...	...	...	...	...	...	...	...	...	...
Boy	...	...	...	...	...	...	...	...	...	...
Gharámí	1 0	1 0	1 0	1 0	1 0	0 1 0	0 1 0	1 0	1 0	1 0
Superior blacksmith	...	...	...	...	...	...	...	...	...	...
Common ,,	...	...	...	...	...	...	...	...	...	...
KOREA STATE.										
Superior mason	...	...	...	...	...	...	...	...	...	...
Common ,,	...	...	...	...	...	...	...	...	...	...
Superior carpenter	...	...	...	...	...	...	...	...	...	...
Common ,,	...	...	...	...	...	...	...	...	...	...
Cooly	...	...	...	...	...	...	...	...	...	...
Woman	...	...	...	...	...	...	...	...	...	...
Boy	...	...	...	...	...	...	...	...	...	...
Gharámí	...	...	...	...	...	...	...	...	...	...
Superior blacksmith	...	...	...	...	...	...	...	...	...	...
Common ,,	...	...	...	...	...	...	...	...	...	...
SURGUJA STATE.										
Superior mason	8 0	8 0	8 0	8 0	8 0	0 8 0	0 8 0	8 0	8 0	8 0
Common ,,	6 0	6 0	6 0	6 0	6 0	0 6 0	0 6 0	6 0	6 0	6 0
Superior carpenter	7 0	7 0	7 0	7 0	7 0	0 7 0	0 7 0	7 0	7 0	7 0
Common ,,	4 0	4 0	4 0	4 0	4 0	0 4 0	0 4 0	4 0	4 0	4 0
Cooly	2 0	2 0	2 0	2 0	2 0	0 2 0	0 2 0	2 0	2 0	2 0
Woman	1 0	1 0	1 0	1 0	1 0	0 1 0	0 1 0	1 0	1 0	1 0
Boy	1 0	1 0	1 0	1 0	1 0	0 1 0	0 1 0	1 0	1 0	1 0
Gharámí	...	...	...	...	...	...	...	...	...	...
Superior blacksmith	8 0	8 0	8 0	8 0	8 0	0 8 0	0 8 0	8 0	8 0	8 0
Common ,,	3 0	3 0	3 0	3 0	3 0	0 3 0	0 3 0	3 0	3 0	3 0
UDAIPUR STATE.										
Superior mason			5					8	8	
Common ,,	2 6	2 6	5		2 6	0 2 6 (a)	0 3 9 (b)	3	3	
Superior carpenter						2 11 0	1 10 9	10	8	
Common ,,	2 6	2 6	5		2 6	0 2 6	0 5 3	5	5	
Cooly	1 0	1 0	1		1 0	0 1 0	0 2 0	2	2	
Woman	1 3	1 3	1		1 3	0 1 3	0 1 6	1	1	
Boy	0 9	0 9	0		0 9	0 0 9	0 0 9	0	0	
Gharámí	2 0	2 0	2		2 0	0 2 0	0 2 0	2	2	
Superior blacksmith	1 6	1 6	1		1 6	0 1 6	0 2 0	2	2	
Common ,,	1 3	1 3	1		1 3	0 1 3	0 1 6	1	1	

N.B.—There are no regular masons or carpenters in Cháng Bhakár State. The women, boys and blacksmiths are paid in kind and an ordinary cooly can work as a gharámí.

(a) A skilled ivory carver from Delhi was engaged on Rs. 80 per month by the late Rájá during this year.

(b) A skilled ivory carver from Delhi was engaged on Rs. 50 per month.

TABLE X.—DAILY WAGES—(concluded.)

FOR	DURING THE LAST FORTNIGHT OF MARCH									
	1893.	1894.	1895.	1896.	1897.	1898.	1899.	1900.	1901.	1902.
	A. P.	A. P.	A. P.	A. P.	A. P.	A. P.	A. P.	A. P.	A. P.	Rs. A. P.
JASHPUR STATE.										
Superior mason	3 6	3 6	3 6	3 6	3 6	3 6	3 6	3 6	3 6	0 3 6
Common ,,	2 6	2 6	2 6	2 6	2 6	2 6	2 6	2 6	2 6	0 2 6
Superior carpenter	4 0	4 0	4 0	4 0	4 0	4 0	4 0	4 0	4 0	0 4 0
Common ,,	2 6	2 6	2 6	2 6	2 6	2 6	2 6	2 6	2 6	0 2 6
Cooly	1 6	1 6	1 6	1 6	1 6	1 6	1 6	1 6	1 6	0 1 6
Woman	1 0	1 0	1 0	1 0	1 0	1 0	1 0	1 0	1 0	0 1 0
Boy	1 3	1 3	1 3	1 3	1 3	1 3	1 3	1 3	1 3	0 1 3
Gharāmi	2 0	2 0	2 0	2 0	2 0	2 0	2 0	2 0	2 0	0 2 0
Superior blacksmith	3 0	3 0	3 0	3 0	3 0	3 0	3 0	3 0	3 0	0 3 0
Common ,,	2 6	2 6	2 6	2 6	2 6	2 6	2 6	2 6	2 6	0 2 6
GANGPUR STATE.										
Superior mason	...	...	...	...	...	...	...	...	8 0	0 8 0
Common ,,	...	...	...	...	...	...	...	...	3 2	0 3 2
Superior carpenter	...	...	...	...	...	...	...	...	10 8	0 10 8
Common ,,	...	...	...	...	...	...	...	...	5 4	0 5 4
Cooly	...	...	...	...	...	...	...	...	2 2	0 2 2
Woman	...	...	...	...	...	...	...	...	1 10	0 1 10
Boy	...	...	...	...	...	...	...	...	1 7	0 1 7
Gharāmi	...	...	...	...	...	...	...	...	2 2	0 2 2
Superior blacksmith	...	...	...	...	...	...	...	...	10 8	0 10 8
Common ,,	...	...	...	...	...	...	...	...	5 4	0 5 4
BONAI STATE.										
Superior mason	...	...	...	...	...	...	...	...	...	1 4 0
Common ,,	10 0	10 0	10 6	11 0	11 0	11 0	1x 6	11 6	12 0	0 12 0
Superior carpenter	...	...	...	...	...	...	...	...	...	...
Common ,,	9 0	9 0	9 0	9 6	9 6	10 0	10 0	10 0	12 0	0 12 0
Cooly	2 0	2 0	2 3	2 6	2 6	2 6	3 0	3 0	3 0	0 3 0
Woman	1 6	1 6	1 6	1 6	1 9	1 9	1 9	1 9	2 0	0 2 0
Boy	1 0	1 0	1 0	1 3	1 6	1 6	1 6	1 6	2 0	0 2 0
Gharāmi	2 3	2 3	2 3	2 6	2 6	2 6	3 0	3 0	3 0	0 3 0
Superior blacksmith	...	...	...	...	...	...	...	...	...	...
Common ,,	3 0	3 0	3 3	3 3	3 6	3 6	3 6	4 0	4 0	0 4 0
KHARSAWAN STATE.										
Superior mason	5 0	5 0	5 0	6 0	6 0	6 0	6 0	6 0	7 0	0 7 0
Common ,,	3 0	3 0	3 0	3 6	4 0	4 0	4 0	4 0	4 0	0 4 0
Superior carpenter	4 0	4 0	4 0	4 0	4 0	4 0	4 0	5 0	5 0	0 5 0
Common ,,	2 6	2 6	2 6	2 6	2 6	2 6	2 6	2 6	2 6	0 2 6
Cooly	2 0	2 0	2 0	2 0	2 0	2 0	2 0	2 0	2 0	0 2 0
Woman	1 6	1 6	1 6	1 6	1 6	1 6	1 6	1 6	1 6	0 1 6
Boy	1 6	1 6	1 6	1 6	1 6	1 6	1 6	1 6	1 6	0 1 6
Gharāmi	2 0	2 0	2 0	2 0	2 0	2 0	2 0	2 0	2 0	0 2 0
Superior blacksmith	4 0	4 0	4 0	5 0	5 0	5 0	5 0	6 0	6 0	0 6 0
Common ,,	2 6	2 6	2 6	2 6	3 0	3 0	3 0	3 0	3 0	0 3 0
SARAIKELA STATE.										
Superior mason	8 0	8 0	13 0	6 0	6 0	6 0	8 0	8 0	8 0	0 8 0
Common ,,	4 0	4 0	6 0	4 0	4 0	4 0	5 0	5 0	5 0	0 5 0
Superior carpenter	4 0	4 0	4 0	4 0	5 0	5 0	5 0	5 0	6 0	0 6 0
Common ,,	3 0	3 0	3 0	3 0	3 0	3 0	4 0	4 0	4 0	0 4 0
Cooly	2 0	2 0	2 0	2 0	2 0	2 3	2 3	2 3	2 3	0 2 3
Woman	1 3	1 3	1 3	1 3	1 6	1 6	1 6	1 6	1 6	0 1 6
Boy	1 0	1 0	1 0	1 3	1 3	1 3	1 6	1 6	1 6	0 1 6
Gharāmi	2 6	2 6	2 6	2 6	2 6	2 6	3 0	3 0	3 0	0 3 0
Superior blacksmith	2 6	2 6	2 6	2 6	2 6	2 6	3 0	3 0	4 0	0 4 0
Common ,,	2 0	2 0	2 0	2 0	2 0	2 6	2 6	3 0	3 0	0 3 0

TABLE XI.—CRIMINAL JUSTICE.

Offence.	Persons convicted or bound over in								
	1898-94.	1894-95.	1895-96.	1896-97.	1897-98.	1898-99.	1899-1900.	1900-01.	1901-02.
1	2	3	4	5	6	7	8	9	10
Total ...	*863*	*875*	*996*	*1,562*	*1,315*	*928*	*1,192*	*1,892*	*1,822*
Offences against public tranquillity.									
Chāng Bhakār ...	...	...	...	...	...	...			
Koreā ...	...	...	...	...	...	...			
Surgujā ...	18	4	14	...	...	3			
Udaipur ...	...	...	...	...	...	...			
Jashpur ...	...	...	6	170	2	...			
Gāngpur ...	12	...	29	...	...	21			
Bonai ...	...	...	...	...	...	...			
Kharsāwān ...	...	...	...	2	6	...			
Saraikelā ...	...	...	...	26	...	9			
Offences affecting the human body.									
Chāng Bhakār ...	13	13	5	8	3	8			
Koreā ...	5	13	12	5	4	5			
Surgujā ...	41	58	36	65	28	29			
Udaipur ...	7	14	7	5	...	6			
Jashpur ...	22	10	15	16	2	18			
Gāngpur ...	18	36	30	14	22	18			
Bonai ...	9	6	28	18	21	21			
Kharsāwān ...	26	6	8	8	4	10			
Saraikelā ...	16	10	21	19	4	23	Separa	Ditto.	Ditto.
Offences against property.									
...	23	35	5	15	19	18			
...	22	18	13	84	47	20			
Surgujā ...	154	213	189	420	567	156			
Udaipur ...	32	29	45	28	40	50			
Jashpur ...	110	51	130	98	84	78			
Gāngpur ...	100	93	191	124	173	148			
Bonai ...	22	45	41	35	9	27			
...	33	23	47	91	65	46			
...	52	60	45	46	100	104			
Other offences against the I. P. C.									
Chāng Bhakār ...	5	20	2	2	...	...			
Koreā ...	15	8	5	22	13	7			
Surgujā ...	20	21	12	30	35	14			
Udaipur ...	4	11	8	7	6	15			
Jashpur ...	15	4	...	117	6	11			
Gāngpur ...	7	6	14	7	1	8			
Bonai ...	23	38	9	8	32	9			
Kharsāwān ...	10	6	1	4	1	3			
Saraikelā ...	16	14	11	15	13	16			
Other offences. *									
Chāng Bhakār ...	...	...	...	...	...	...	20	44	57
Koreā ...	...	...	...	...	...	...	53	82	41
Surgujā ...	2	3	4	3	1	5	375	755	647
Udaipur ...	3	2	10	5	3	5	48	70	62
Jashpur ...	...	...	...	12	...	5	77	215	258
Gāngpur ...	...	...	...	...	...	6	276	459	373
Bonai ...	...	...	...	...	...	...	49	38	64
Kharsāwān ...	2	...	...	7	2	2	99	66	105
Saraikelā ...	6	5	3	26	2	9	195	163	215

* The figures for 1899-1900, 1900-01 and 1901-02 include offences against the Indian Penal Code.

TABLE XII.—WORK OF THE CRIMINAL COURTS.

NAME OF COURT.	STATE.	NUMBER OF PERSONS UNDER TRIAL DURING—								
		1893-94.	1894-95.	1895-96.	1896-97.	1897-98.	1898-99.	1899-1900.	1900-01.	1901-02.
	ORIGINAL ...	*43*	*30*	*8*	*35*	*149*	*43*	*34*	*65*	*43*
Commissioner's court.	Chāng Bhakār ...	1	1	...	...	9	2	...	2	
	Koreā ...	...	...	...	...	...	1	...	2	...
	Surgujā ...	...	...	...	3	12	...	...	1	2
	Udaipur ...	...	...	...	...	...	...	...	...	...
	Jashpur ...	...	...	...	...	1	...	1	...	...
	Gāngpur ...	...	...	...	...	27	6	...	39	...
	Bonai ...	...	...	...	...	8	12	1	1	5
	Kharsāwān ...	...	...	...	...	...	...	...	...	
	Saraikelā ...	...	...	...	...	...	7	...	...	...
Sessions court.	Chāng Bhakār ...	...	...	...	...	...	...	...	...	1
	Koreā ...	...	3	5	14	19	...	4	...	1
	Surgujā ...	14	17	...	4	2	2	4	...	...
	Udaipur ...	...	1	...	4	4	...	...	1	2
	Jashpur ...	2	3	2	...	3	3	6	...	3
	Gāngpur ...	26	1	1	2	57	9	15	11	23
	Bonai ...	...	1	...	...	1	1	3	5	...
	Kharsāwān ...	...	...	...	1	...	...	...	...	...
	Saraikelā ...	...	3	...	7	6	...	...	3	1
	APPELLATE ...	*28*	*23*	*28*	*38*	*55*	*65*	*89*	*71*	*81*
Commissioner's court.	Chāng Bhakār ...	...	...	...	...	...	...	...	...	...
	Koreā ...	1	1	...	1	5	2	3	3	8
	Surgujā ...	2	...	1	4	1	2			21
	Udaipur ...	...	...	...	...	...	...	...	...	...
	Jashpur ...	...	...	...	2	2	...	2	2	3
	Gāngpur ...	9	5	2	3	2	12	17	18	23
	Bonai ...	2	...	2	1	6	1		2	1
	Kharsāwān ...	1	...	...	1	5	5	.	4	3
	Saraikelā ...	2	1	5	4	4	4	9	7	1
Deputy Commissioner's court.	Koirā Dehāt in Bonai ...	...	2	...	...	...	...	...		
	Kharsāwān ...	4	6	6	11	7	8	9	.	
	Saraikelā ...	7	8	12	1	23	31	45	27	14

TABLE XIII.—CIVIL JUSTICE.

Year.	Name of Court.	Number of civil suits in:								
		Chāng Bhakūr.	Koreā.	Surgujā.	Udaipur.	Jashpur.	Gāngpur.	Bonai.	Kharsāwān.	Saraikelā.
1	2	3	4	5	6	7	8	9	10	11
1893-94	Court of the State concerned.	4	6	100	22	30	90	10	140	277
1894-95		21	5	94	8	34	47	11	110	246
1895-96		9	12	70	8	28	123	21	152	239
1896-97		5	4	91	1	43	94	7	175	204
1897-98		6	21	56	4	11	39	4	138	246
1898-99		14	16	37	2	43	121	49	120	172
1899-1900		4	20	43	8	20	306	30	138	210
1900-01		3	52	88	11	60	232	10	200	150
1901-02		16	17	90	13	99	270	9	161	300
1902-03		14	24	106	24	80	273	122	197	356
1893-94	Commissioner's Court.	...	...	...	...	...	...	...	...	...
1894-95		...	...	...	...	...	...	...	...	...
1895-96		...	...	...	...	...	...	...	...	...
1896-97		...	...	...	...	...	...	...		...
1897-98		...	...	1	1	3	11	8		...
1898-99		2	8	...	1	...	1	...		...
1899-1900		2	1	4	1	...	7	4		...
1900-01		...	5	...	3	...	8	1	...	...
1901-02		...	...	1	...	2	2	4	...	...
1902-03		...	2	1	...	...	6	2	...	...
1893-94	Singhbhum Deputy Commissioner's Court for Saraikelā and Kharsāwān only.	...	...	...	...	...	...	...	3	54
1894-95		...	...	...	...	...	...	...	10	3
1895-96		...	...	...	...	...	...	...	8	4
896-97		...	...	...	...	...	...	...	29	10
1897-98		...	...	...	...	...	...	...	6	1
1898-99		...	...	...	...	...	...	...	17	4
1899-1900		...	...	...	...	...	...	...	4	5
1900-01		...	...	...	...	...	...	...	63	1
1901-02		...	...	...	...	...	...	...	4	62
1902-03		...	...	...	...	...	...	...	64	2

TABLE XIV.—CIVIL JUSTICE : APPEALS.

Class of Courts.	State.	Total number of appeals in								
		1893-94.	1894-95.	1895-96.	1896-97.	1897-98.	1898-99.	1899-1900.	1900-01.	1901-02.
Commissioner's court.	Chāng Bhakūr	...	...	...	...	...	1	1	...	...
	Koreā	...	...	2	1	9	9	1	6	10
	Surgujā	5	6	3	4	3	4	6	1	7
	Udaipur	...	...	...	...	...	...	...	...	...
	Jashpur	10	10	8	8	1	2	3	6	15
	Gāngpur	...	...	...	...	19	24	32	31	49
	Bonai	...	...	10	11	4	...	2	2	1
	Kharsāwān	7	5	8	14	13	6	15	4	7
	Saraikelā	19	15	24	16	6	8	11	12	16
Deputy Commissioner's court.	Kharsāwān	9	13	22	38	27	11	17	25	25
	Saraikelā	30	34	42	29	26	19	33	42	31

TABLE XV.—FINANCE (TOTAL

Serial No.	STATE.	1892-93.	1893-94.	1894-95.
			Rs.	Rs.
1	Chāng Bhakār ...		3,800	3,800
2	Koreā ... ... ,		6,796	8,488
3	Surgujā		38,471	38,471
4	Udaipur		15,917	15,917
5	Jashpur		24,718	28,456
6	Gāngpur		27,401	32,184
7	Bonai		11,067	11,249
8	Kharsāwān		18,873	19,712
9	Saraikelā		65,138	65,288

TABLE XVI.—LAND REVENUE AND CESSES

(Compiled from information supplied by the

Serial No.	STATE.	1892-93.	1893-94.	1894-95.
1	Chāng Bhakār ... ... ,			
2	Koreā			
3	Surgujā			
4	Udaipur			
5	Jashpur			
6	Gāngpur			
7	Bonai			
8	Kharsāwān ... ... ,			
9	Saraikelā			

REVENUE FROM ALL SOURCES).

1895-96.	1896-97.	1897-98.	1898-99.	1899-1900.	1900-01.	1901-02.	Serial No.
Rs.	Rs.	Rs.	Rs.	Rs.	Rs.	Rs.	
3,800	3,800	...					1
9,445	6,050	8,877					2
38,471	37,171	29,044					3
16,862	15,662						4
29,184	34,480	38,341					5
38,213	53,696	58,050					6
14,257	14,257	15,425					7
19,712	23,467	24,564					8
68,204	66,727	67,429	7				9

(TOTAL CURRENT DEMAND FROM ALL SOURCES).

Commissioner, Chota Nāgpur Division.)

1895-96.	1896-97.	1897-98.	1898-99.	1899-1900.	1900-01.	1901-02.	Serial No.
Rs.	Rs.	Rs.	Rs.	Rs.	Rs.	Rs.	
1,400	1,400	...	1,661				
3,430	2,125	3,772					
31,289	31,289	25,893					
11,415	11,111						
23,150	23,336	25,410					
4,606	14,606	14,606					
0,623	10,623	10,623					
14,000	14,218	14,269					
47,629	48 644	49,548	49,548				

TABLE XVII.—

Compiled from information supplied by the

Serial No.	STATE.	EXCISE ARTICLES: RECEIPTS FROM.				1892-93.	1893-94.	1894-95.
						Rs.	Rs.	Rs.
1	Chāng Bhakār.	Country spirits	...	...	...	50	50	50
		Opium	...	...	...	...	...	...
		Gānjā	...	...	...	...	...	...
		Miscellaneous	...	...	...	...	...	...
			TOTAL		...	50	50	50
2	Koreā ...	Country spirits	...	...	...	249	488	376
		Opium	...	...	...	...	...	...
		Gānjā	...	...	...	...	...	...
		Miscellaneous	...	...	...	...	...	...
			TOTAL		...	249	488	376
3	Surgujā	Country spirits	...	...	...	7,190	6,700	5,262
		Opium	...	...	...	1	...	...
		Gānjā	...	...	...	...	...	...
		Miscellaneous	...	...	...	...	...	...
			TOTAL		...	7,191	6,700	5,262
4	Udaipur	Country spirits	...	...	...	701	1,462	1,759
		Opium	...	...	...	...	...	...
		Gānjā	...	...	...	...	...	...
		Miscellaneous	...	...	...	...	...	...
			TOTAL		...	701	1,462	1,759
5	Jashpur	Country spirits		...	..	1,114	1,163	1,163
		Opium	...	...	...	1	...	...
		Gānjā	...	...	...	...	...	...
		Miscellaneous	...	...	...	...	...	...
			TOTAL		..	1,115	1,163	1,163
6	Gāngpur	Country spirits	...	...	...	4,333	4,333	4,333
		Opium	...	...	...	2	...	...
		Gānjā	...	...	...	...	...	...
		Miscellaneous			...	...	...	...
			TOTAL		...	4,335	4,333	4,333
7	Bonai ...	Country spirits	...	...	...	...	170	214
		Opium	...	...	...	...	...	...
		Gānjā	...	...	...	...	...	...
		Miscellaneous	...	...	...	...	35	41
			TOTAL		...	...	205	255
8	Kharsā- wān.	Country spirits	...	...	...	2,900	3,200	3,600
		Opium	...		...	1	960	800
		Gānjā	...	...	...	...	...	...
		Miscellaneous			...	...	...	...
			TOTAL		...	2,901	4,160	4,400
9	Saraikelā	Country spirits	...	...	...	6,850	7,175	6,600
		Opium	...	...	...	4	808	808
		Gānjā	...	...	...	404	404	404
		Miscellaneous	...	...	...	50	50	50
			TOTAL		...	7,308	8,437	7,862

TABLES.—XVIII to

EXCISE.

Commissioner, Chota Nāgpur Division.)

1895-96.	1896-97.	1897-98.	1898-99.	1899-1900.	1900-01.	1901-02.	Serial No.
Rs.	Rs.	Rs.	Rs.	Rs.	Rs.	Rs.	
80	60	70	70	70	70	109 ⎫	
...	...	...	...	...	...	... ⎬	
...	...	...	...	...	...	...	
...	...	...	...	...	...	... ⎭	
80	*60*	*70*	*70*	*70*	*70*	*109*	
303	237	210	574	584	560	580 ⎫	
...	...	...	...	...	...	... ⎬	
...	...	...	...	...	...	...	
...	...	...	...	...	...	... ⎭	
303	*237*	*210*	*574*	*584*	*560*	*580*	
7,330	7,244	7,565	9,341	9,354	3,253	8,896 ⎫	
...	...	...	...	...	...	... ⎬	
...	...	...	...	...	...	331	
...	...	...	10	15	11	18 ⎭	
7,330	*7,244*	*7,565*	*9,351*	*9,369*	*3,264*	*9,245*	
1,800	1,797	1,575	1,532	1,125	...	930 ⎫	
...	...	...	...	...	...	... ⎬	
...	...	...	...	...	...	...	
...	...	...	...	...	...	... ⎭	
1,800	*1,797*	*1,575*	*1,532*	*1,125*	...	*930*	
1,170	1,967	2,112	2,199	3,319	3,763	4,174 ⎫	
...	...	...	...	...	...	310 ⎬	
...	...	...	...	...	...	...	
...	...	...	...	...	...	... ⎭	
1,170	*1,967*	*2,112*	*2,199*	*3,319*	*3,763*	*4,484*	
4,383	6,358	8,406	13,536	13,484	24,061	35,317 ⎫	
...	...	...	3,591	5,936	5,945	6,869 ⎬	
...	...	...	229	300	...	...	
...	...	...	...	...	50	123 ⎭	
4,383	*6,358*	*8,406*		*19,720*	*30,065*	*42,208*	
480	945	935		1,072	1,310	1,330 ⎫	
60	60	...		350	500	500 ⎬	
...	...	...		...	...	...	
40	40	51		51	51	51 ⎭	
580	*1,045*	*986*		*1,473*	*1,861*	*1,881*	
3,600	4,600	4,315		5,006	3,475	3,960 ⎫	
800	500	600		700	700	1,005 ⎬	8
...	...	...	...	...	...	...	
...	...	...	...	...	...	... ⎭	
4,400	*5,100*	*4,915*	*5,700*	*5,706*	*4,175*	*4,965*	
11,769	11,042	8,508	8,012	9,226	7,781	9,440 ⎫	
1,000	1,500	1,280	1,350	1,365	1,345	1,350 ⎬	9
450	553	460	650	656	655	650	
60	72	80	...	...	...	... ⎭	
13,279	*13,167*	*10,328*	*10,012*	*11,247*	*9,781*	*11,440*	

XXI.—(Blank.)

(Compiled t

Serial No.	NAME OF MUNICIPALITY.	RECEIPTS AND EXPENDITURE.	19
	Kharsáwán (a)	{ Receipts — { Expenditure —	
	Saraikelá	{ Receipts — { Expenditure ...	

Serial No.	STATE.		
		TOTAL	
1	Cháng Bhakár	... ...	
2	Koreá	... ...	
3	Surgujá	... ...	
4	Udaipur	... ...	
5	Jashpur	... ...	
6	Gángpur	... ...	
7	Bonai	... ...	
8	Kharsáwán	... ...	
9	Saraikelá	... ...	

Serial No.	NAME AND CLASS OF JAIL.
1	Cháng Bhakár 3rd cl
2	Koreá Jail ...
3	Surgujá .. ...
4	Udaipur State Jai!
5	Jashpur State Jai'
6	Gángpur District
7	Bonai Sub-Jail
8	Kharsáwán Jail
9	Saraikelá Politi

MUNICIPALITIES.

Commissioner, Chota Nāgpur Division.)

1895-96.	1896-97,	1897-98.	1898-99,	1899-1900.	1900-01.	1901-02.	Serial No.
Rs.	Rs. A. P.	Rs. A. P.	Rs. A. P.	Rs. A. P.	Rs. A. P.	Rs. A. P.	
...	...	...	...	...	...	516 0 0	}1
...					...	388 0 0	
404	496 0 3	524 9 9	467 2 0	582 4 0	475 12 6	463 7 3	}2
404	496 0 3	524 9 9	467 2 0	582 4 0	475 12 6	463 7 3	

in Kharsāwān till 1901.

OF POLICE, 1902-03.

Commissioner, Chota Nāgpur Division.)

RURAL POLICE.				Serial No.
Under Act VI (B.C.) of 1870.		Under Regulation XX of 1817.	Chākrān, Ghātwāl, etc.	
Dafādārs.	Chankidārs.			
...	...		...	1
...	...	...	...	2
...	...	...	...	3
...	...		...	4
...	...		...	5
...	...		...	6
...	...			7
...	...	...	...	8
...	...		...	9

police have not been supplied.

JAILS.

Commissioner, Chota Nāgpur Division.)

AVERAGE NUMBER OF PRISONERS IN								Serial No.
1895.	1896.	1897.	1898.	1899.	1900.	1901.	1902,	
35·00	22·00	12·00	13·00	14·00	6·00	27	72·	1
2·00	36·00	5·00	8·00	8·00	15·00	11	7·	2
0·50	0·90	1·33	0·45	0·70	1·20	0·	0·	3
...	...	...	...	...	...	40	36·	4
...	...	...	...	41·63	49·64	60	80·	5
...	...	...	...	...	53·66	47	40·	6
2·00	5·00	2·00	3·00	3·00	3·00	4·	6·	7
...	...	...	...	...	...	4·00	9·00	8
...	...	...	...	...	...	12·00	13·00	9

were not properly kept before 1900.
before 1900.

TABLE XXV.—EDUCATION :

(Compiled from the Tabulation Register to Census

Serial No.	State.	Principal Religions.	Total Popula	
			Total.	Male.
		2	3	
	Total ...{	Hindu ... ... Musalmān ... Animist	615,454 8,614 375,478	312,248 4,521 *89,019
	Chāng Bhakār ... ...{	Hindu ... ... Musalmān ... Animist ...	19,516 31 1	9,986 16 1
2	Koreā ... ...{	Hindu ... ... Musalmān ... Animist	24,430 288 10,395	12,526 171 5,251
3	Surgujā ... ...{	Hindu ... .. Musalmān ... Animist	204,228 *3,909 142,783	103,408 2,062 72,490
4	Udaipur ... ...{	Hindu ... ... Musalmān ... Animist	41,373 131 3,897	21,060 64 1,983
5	Jashpur ... ...{	Hindu ... ... Musalmān ... Animist	69,473 1,154 61,475	35,360 596 30,787
6	Gāngpur ... ...{	Hindu ... Musalmān ... Animist	146,549 1,640 88,949	74,717 901 44,971
7	Bonai ... ...{	Hindu ... Musalmān ... Animist	26,371 69 11,745	13,712 46 6,193
	Kharsāwān ... ...{	Hindu ... .. Musalmān ... Animist	19,864 399 16,277	9,696 185 7,887
	Saraikelā ... ...{	Hindu ... ... Musalmān ... Animist	63,650 913 39,956	31,583 480 19,456

EXCISE.

Commissioner, Chota Nágpur Division.)

1895-96.	1896-97.	1897-98.	1898-99.	1899-1900.	1900-01.	1901-02.	Serial No.
Rs.	Rs.	Rs.	Rs.	Rs.	Rs.	Rs.	
80	60	70	70	70	70	109	
...	...	...	...	...	...	...	
...	...	...	...	...	...	...	
...	...	...	...	...	...	...	
80	*60*	*70*	*70*	*70*	*70*	*109*	
303	237	210	574	584	560	580	
...	...	...	...	...	...	...	
...	...	...	...	...	...	...	2
...	...	...	...	...	...	...	
303	*237*	*210*	*574*	*584*	*560*	*580*	
7,330	7,244	7,565	9,341	9,354	3,253	8,896	
...	...	...	...	...	...	331	3
...	...	...	...	...	...	18	
...	...	...	10	15	11		
7,330	*7,244*	*7,565*	*9,351*	*9,369*	*3,264*	*9,245*	
1,800	1,797	1,575	1,532	1,125	...	930	
...	...	...	...	...	...	...	
...	...	...	...	...	...	...	
...	...	...	...	...	...	...	
1,800	*1,797*	*1,575*	*1,532*	*1,125*	*...*	*930*	
1,170	1,967	2,112	2,199	3,319	3,763	4,174	
...	...	...	...	...	...	310	5
...	...	...	...	...	...	...	
...	...	...	...	...	...	...	
1,170	*1,967*	*2,112*	*2,199*	*3,319*	*3,763*	*4,484*	
4,333	6,358	8,406	13,536	13,484	24,061	35,217	
...	...	...	3,591	5,936	5,945	6,868	6
...	...	...	229	300	...	123	
...	...	...	...	...	59		
4,333	*6,358*	*8,406*	*17,356*	*19,720*	*30,065*	*42,208*	
480	945	935	850	1,072	1,310	1,330	
60	60	...	70	350	500	500	7
...	...	...	...	...	...	...	
40	40	51	51	51	51	51	
580	*1,045*	*986*	*971*	*1,473*	*1,861*	*1,881*	
3,600	4,600	4,315	5,000	5,006	3,475	3,960	
800	500	600	700	700	700	1,005	8
...	...	...	...	...	...	...	
...	...	...	...	...	...	...	
4,400	*5,100*	*4,915*	*5,700*	*5,706*	*4,175*	*4,965*	
11,769	11,042	8,508	8,012	9,226	7,781	9,440	
1,000	1,500	1,280	1,350	1,365	1,345	1,350	9
450	553	460	650	656	655	650	
60	72	80	...	...	...	...	
13,279	*13,167*	*10,328*	*10,012*	*11,247*	*9,781*	*11,440*	

XXI.—(Blank.)

TABLE XXII.—

(Compiled from information supplied by the

Serial No.	NAME OF MUNICIPALITY.	RECEIPTS AND EXPENDITURE.	1892-93.	1893-94.	1894-95.
			Rs.	Rs.	Rs.
1	Kharsāwān (a) ...	{ Receipts ... { Expenditure ...	... ...	... ...	
2	Saraikelā	{ Receipts ... { Expenditure ...	400 400	404 404	408 408

(a) There was no municipality

TABLE XXIII.—DISTRIBUTION

(Compiled from information supplied by the

Serial No.	STATE.	STRENGTH OF POLICE.		Number of Village Unions.
		Officers.	Constables.	
	TOTAL ..	96	394	...
1	Chāng Bhakār	4	7	...
2	Koreā	3	10	...
3	Surgujā	23	102	...
4	Udaipur	7	47	...
5	Jashpur	12	35	...
6	Gāngpur	28	131	...
7	Bonai	9	28	...
8	Kharsāwān	3	12	...
9	Saraikelā	7	22	...

Details as to numbers of village

TABLE XXIV.—

(Compiled from information supplied by the

Serial No.	NAME AND CLASS OF JAIL.	ACCOMMODATION FOR			DAILY	
		Total.	Males.	Females.	1893.	1894.
1	Chāng Bhakār 3rd class Jail	10	8	2	...	...
2	Koreā Jail	7	7	...	7·00	3·00
3	Surgujā „	5	4	1	0·30	0·46
4	Udaipur State Jail ...	60	50	10	...	...
5	Jashpur State Jail, 3rd class	102	97	5	...	...
6	Gāngpur District Jail* ...	54	50	4	...	...
7	Bonai Sub-Jail	50	50	...	1· 0	1·00
8	Kharsāwān Jail	11	8	3	...	...
9	Saraikelā Political Jail†	32	22	10	...	...

* Columns 5 to 11 have been left blank, as the registers, etc.,
† There was no ail

MUNICIPALITIES.

Commissioner, Chota Nāgpur Division.)

1895–96.	1896–97,	1897–98.	1898–99,	1899–1900,	1900–01.	1901–02.	Serial No.
Rs.	Rs. A. P.	Rs. A. P.	Rs. A. P.	Rs. A. P.	Rs. A. P.	Rs. A. P.	
...		...	...		...	516 0 0	}1
...	...	...	...	...	...	388 0 0	
404	496 0 3	524 9 9	467 2 0	582 4 0	475 12 6	463 7 3	}2
404	496 0 3	524 9 9	467 2 0	582 4 0	475 12 6	463 7 3	

in Kharsāwān till 1901.

OF POLICE, 1902–03.

Commissioner, Chota Nāgpur Division.)

RURAL POLICE.				Serial No.
Under Act VI (B.C.) of 1870.		Under Regulation XX of 1817.	Chākrān, Ghātwāl, etc.	
Dafādārs.	Chankidārs.			
...	...		...	1
...	...			2
...	...		...	3
...	...			4
...	...		...	5
	...		...	6
		...	...	7
...	...		...	8
...	...		...	9

police have not been supplied.

JAILS.

Commissioner, Chota Nāgpur Division.)

AVERAGE NUMBER OF PRISONERS IN

1895.	1896.	1897.	1898.	1899.	1900.	1901.	1902.	Serial No.
35·00	22·00	12·00	13·00	14·00	6·00	27·00	72·00	1
2·00	36·00	5·00	2·00	8·00	15·00	11·00	7·00	2
0·50	0·90	1·33	0·46	0·70	1·20	0·96	0·75	3
...	...	...	...	...	...	40·05	36·51	4
...	...	...	...	41·63	49·64	60·63	80·72	5
...	...	...	...	...	53·66	47·46	40·06	6
2·00	5·00	2·00	3·00	3·00	3·00	4·00	6·00	7
...	...	...	...	...	...	4·10	9·60	8
...	...	...	...	...	...	12·00	13·00	9

were not properly kept before 1900.
before 1900.

STATISTICAL TABLES.

TABLE XXV.—EDUCATION :

(Compiled from the Tabulation Register to Census

Serial No.	STATE.	PRINCIPAL RELIGIONS.	TOTAL POPULA	
			Total.	Male.
		2	3	
	TOTAL ... {	Hindu ...	*615,454*	*312,248*
		Musalmān ...	*8,614*	*4,521*
		Animist	*375,478*	*`89,019*
	Chāng Bhakār ... ... {	Hindu	19,516	9,986
		Musalmān .	31	16
		Animist	1	1
2	Koreā ... ... {	Hindu	24,430	12,526
		Musalmān ..	288	171
		Animist	10,395	5,351
3	Surgujā ... ... {	Hindu	204,228	103,406
		Musalmān ...	13,999	2,062
		Animist	142,783	72,490
2	Udaipur ... ● ... {	Hindu	41,373	21,060
		Musalmān ...	131	64
		Animist	3,897	1,983
5	Jashpur ... ... {	Hindu	69,473	35,260
		Musalmān ...	1,154	596
		Animist	61,475	30,787
	Gāngpur ... ... {	Hindu	146,549	74,717
		Musalmān ...	1,640	901
		Animist	88,949	44,971
	Bonai ... ... {	Hindu	26,371	13,712
		Musalmān ...	69	46
		Animist	11,745	6,193
	Kharsāwān ... ... {	Hindu	19,864	9,696
		Musalmān ...	399	185
		Animist	16,277	7,887
	Saraikelā ... {	Hindu	63,650	31,883
		Musalmān ...	913	480
		Animist	39,956	19,456

PROPORTION OF LITERATES.

Table VIII and from the Provincial Table II of 1901.)

TION.	LITERATE.			PERCENTAGE OF LITERATES TO TOTAL POPULATION.			Serial No.
Female.	Total.	Male.	Female.	Total.	Male.	Female.	
5	6	7	8	9	10	11	
303,206	7,516	7,092	424	1·2	2·3	0·1	
4,093	420	411	9	5·0	9·7	0·2	
186,459	295	271	24	0·1	0·1	0·0	.
9,530	46	45	1	0·2	0·5	0·0 }	
15	1	1	...	3·2	6·2	... }	1
...	...	...	...	...	...	...	
11,904	62	57	5	0·3	0·5	0·0 }	
117	13	11	2	4·5	6·4	1·7 }	2
5,144	9	7	2	0·1	0·1	0·0 }	
100,820	738	726	10	0·4	0·7	0·0 }	
1,937	136	136	...	3·4	6·6	... }	
70,293	39	35	4	0·0	0·0	0·0 }	
20,313	207	179	28	0·5	0·8	0·1 }	
57	5	5	...	4·1	7·8	... }	
1,914	17	9	8	0·4	0·5	0·4 }	
34,213	753	671	82	1·1	1·9	0·2 }	
558	58	58	...	5·0	9·7	... }	
30,688	49	47	2	0·1	0·2	0·0 }	
71,832	2,904	2,748	156	2·0	3·7	0·2 }	
739	97	96	1	5·9	10·7	0·1 }	6
45,978	76	69	7	0·1	0·2	0·0 }	
12,659	339	317	22	1·3	2·3	0·2 }	
23	16	15	1	23·2	32·6	4·3 }	7
5,552	5	4	1	0·0	0·1	0·0 }	
10,168	976	916	60	4·9	9·4	0·6 }	
214	38	36	2	9·5	19·5	0·9 }	
8,390	43	43	...	0·3	0·5	... }	
31,767	1,491	1,431	60	2·3	4·5	0·2 }	
433	56	53	3	6·1	11·0	0·7 }	
20,500	57	57	...	0·1	0·2	... }	

STATISTICAL TABLES.

TABLE XXVI.—EDUCATION : NUMBER

(Compiled from information supplied by the

Serial No.	NAME OF STATE.	Number of	1892–93.	1893–94.	1894–95.
*	TOTAL	...	37 953	52 1,408	69 1,747
1	Chāng Bhakār	...	1 15	1 5	4 46
2	Koreā ...	...	... ...	... ...	3 44
3	Surgujā ...	...	6 156	7 292	17 382
4	Udaipur	...	3 107	4 60	4 77
5	Jashpur	...	2 36	5 69	6 196
6	Gāngpur ...	...	1 15	7 224	11 377
7	Bonai ...	...	... ...	10 299	4 121
8	Kharsāwān	...	10 194	7 204	5 121
9	Saraikelā ...	...	14 430	11 255	15 383

TABLE XXVII.—EDUCATION: PUBLIC INSTITUTIONS

(Compiled from information supplied by the

Serial No.	NAME OF STATE.	SECONDARY.						PUBLIC PRIM	
		High English.		Middle English.		Middle Vernacular.		Upper Primary.	
		Schools.	Scholars.	Schools.	Scholars.	Schools.	Scholars.	Schools.	Scholars.
		2	3	4	5	6	7	8	9
	TOTAL	...	...	3	149	1	70	12	337
1	Chāng Bhakár ...	...	...	...	...	...	...	...	...
2	Koreā	...	...	...	...	...	...	...	...
3	Surgujā	...	...	...	...	...	...	...	...
4	Udaipur ...	...	...	...	...	...	...	...	...
5	Jashpur ...	...	...	...	...	...	...	...	...
6	Gāngpur ...	...	...	1	7	1	70	9	202
7	Bonai	...	...	...	...	...	...	...	...
8	Kharsāwān ...	...	...	1	67	...	...	...	...
9	Saraikelā ...	...	...	1	75	...	...	3	135

* Class of 12 institutions

OF INSTITUTIONS AND SCHOLARS.
Commissioner, Chota Nagpur Division.)

Each cell shows institutions (top number) over scholars (bottom number).

1895–96.	1896–97.	1897–98.	1898–99.	1899–1900.	1900–01.	1901–02.	Serial No.
52 / 1,226	64 / 1,483	79 / 1,626	70 / 1,307	64 / 1,398	72 / 1,584	97 / 2,029	
4 / 53	4 / 37	4 / 28	4 / 28	4 / 28	4 / 28	1 / 7	1
3 / 31	2 / 22	... / ...	... / ...	1 / 6	2 / 21	... / ...	2
17 / 327	17 / 301	17 / 351	11 / 89	11 / 177	10 / 180	38 / 604	3
4 / 78	4 / 80	5 / 77	2 / 42	2 / 41	... / ...	4 / 99	4
7 / 160	7 / 191	11 / 253	13 / 246	9 / 183	9 / 163	8 / 173	5
10 / 381	10 / 312	10 / 259	9 / 265	9 / 303	11 / 300	11 / 279	6
2 / 17	2 / 18	4 / 53	2 / 28	2 / 22	3 / 44	3 / 45	7
4 / 143	7 / 142	5 / 109	5 / 194	2 / 132	9 / 308	8 / 250	8
1 / 36	11 / 380	23 / 496	24 / 415	24 / 506	24 / 340	24 / 572	9

AND SCHOLARS THEREIN IN 1901–02.
Commissioner, Chota Nagpur Division.)

INSTITUTIONS.						PRIVATE INSTITUTIONS.		GRAND TOTAL.		Serial No.
ARY.		SPECIAL.		TOTAL.						
Lower Primary.										
Schools.	Scholars.	Schools.	Scholars.	Schools.	Scholars.	Schools.	Scholars.	Schools.	Scholars.	
10	11	12	13	14	15	16	17	18	19	
13	377	1	9	42*	1,167	55	862	97	2,029	
...	...	...	...	1*	7	...	...	1	7	1
...	...	...	...	...	...	...	...	...	...	2
...	...	...	...	...	...	38	604	38	604	3
4	99	...	...	4	99	...	...	4	99	4
...	...	...	...	8*	173	...	...	8	173	5
...	...	...	...	11	279	...	...	11	279	6
...	...	...	...	3*	45	...	...	3	45	7
2	122	1	9	4	198	4	52	8	250	8
7	156	...	...	11	366	13	206	24	572	9

with 225 scholars not known.

TABLE XXVIII.—EXPENDITURE

(Compiled from information supplied by the

Serial No.	NAME OF STATE.	Paid by the state.
		2
		Rs.
	TOTAL	3,355
1	Chāng Bhakār	50
2	Koreā	
3	Surgujā	471
4	Udaipur	
5	Jashpur	606
6	Gāngpur	
7	Bonai	46
8	Kharsāwān	929
9	Saraikelā	1,253

TABLE XXIX.—

(Compiled from information supplied by the

Serial No.	NAME OF DISPENSARY.	Class.	INDOOR AND OUTDOOR ATTENDANCE.		1892-93.	1893-94.
1	Bisrāmpur Dispensary in Surgujā	I ...	Indoor ... Outdoor ...		... 79	... 1,335
2	Dharmjaygarh Dispensary in Udaipur.	I ...	Indoor ... Outdoor .			... 297
3	Saraikelā	I ...	Indoor ... Outdoor ...		... ...	... ...
4	Kharsāwān	I ...	Indoor ... Outdoor ...		... ...	... ...
5	Gāngpur	I ...	Indoor ... Outdoor ...		... ...	... ...
6	Jashpur	I ...	Indoor ... Outdoor ...		... ...	... ..
7	Bonai	I ...	Indoor ... Outdoor ...		... ...	... ...

ON PUBLIC INSTRUCTION IN 1901-02.

Commissioner, Chota Nāgpur Division.)

EXPENDITURE.		Serial No.
From other sources.	Total expenditure.	
:	±	
Rs.	Rs.	
1,343	4,698	
	50	1
	.. 471	2 / 3
42	.. 648	4 / 5
	... 46	6 / 7
97	1,026	8
1,204	2,457	9

DISPENSARIES.

Commissioner, Chota Nāgpur Division.)

NUMBER OF PATIENTS.								Serial No.
1894-95.	1895-96.	1896-97.	1897-98.	1898-99.	1899-1900.	1900-01.	1901-02.	
14	...	...	...	...	...	...	...	
630	952	...	372	660	571	1,180	462 }	
...	2	1	...	...	...	...	4 }	2
229	481	587	...	89	165	277	6,848 }	
...	...	...	...	...	...	...	... }	3
186	416	417	447	744	849	851	867 }	
...	...	...	...	...	...	...	...	
72	88	...	...	49	109	106	136 }	
...	...	...	...	...	...	...	...	
...	...	976	1,228	1,320	1,427	1,592	1,988 }	5
...	...	...	...	...	...	9	50 }	
...	...	858	...	...	1,702	1,523	3,636 }	6
...	...	...	...	...	...	...	...	
...	...	...	...	...	739	1,656	1,530 }	7

TABLE XXX.—

Serial No.	PARTICULARS.	1892-93.	1893-94.	1894-95.
	PRIMARY SUCCESSFUL VACCINATIONS.			
	TOTAL		15,280	24,639
1	Chäng Bhakär		...	273
2	Koreä		791	602
3	Surgujä		7,022	7,507
4	Udaipur		...	1,823
5	Jashpur		2,262	3,645
6	Gängpur		1,930	5,551
7	Bonai		...	236
8	Kharsäwän		701	1,249
9	Saraikelä		2,574	3,753
	SUCCESSFUL REVACCINATIONS.			
	TOTAL	18	...	1
10	Chäng Bhakär	...	...	
11	Koreä	...		
12	Surgujä	...		
13	Udaipur		...	...
14	Jashpur	...	...	
15	Gängpur		...	...
16	Bonai	...		
17	Kharsäwän	18		
18	Saraikelä			1
	NUMBER OF SUCCESSFUL VACCINATIONS PER 1,000 OF THE POPULATION. (FOR ALL STATES) ...		19·3	
19	Chäng Bhakär		21·8	
20	Koreä		21·8	
21	Surgujä		21·6	
22	Udaipur			
23	Jashpur		19·9	
24	Gängpur		10·1	
25	Bonai		...	
26	Kharsäwän		19·8	
27	Saraikelä...		27·4	